For:

TRADITION!

JEWISH WISDOM
for
EVERYDAY LIFE

Edited by Suzanne Siegel Zenkel

Illustrations taken from serigraphs by Lydie Egosi
Design by Sims and Stern

PETER PAUPER PRESS, INC.
WHITE PLAINS, NEW YORK

To Rabbi Jack Stern and Rabbi David Stern,
for your wisdom and your friendship

Text copyright © 1996
Peter Pauper Press, Inc.
202 Mamaroneck Avenue
White Plains, NY 10601
Illustrations copyright © 1996
Lydie Egosi
ISBN 0-88088-862-8
Printed in Singapore
7 6 5 4 3 2 1

Tradition is not the grit and the rust in the wheels of progress. Not infrequently it is the oil that lubricates those wheels.

—*Rabbi Joseph Lookstein*

$\mathscr{C}$ONTENTS

INTRODUCTION

*I*n 1916, Maxim Gorky, who was not of the Jewish faith, wrote: "I believe that Jewish wisdom is more all-human and universal than any other; and this not only because of its immemorial age, not only because it is the firstborn, but also because of the powerful humaneness that saturates it, because of its high estimate of man." This sensitive insight attests that there is much to appreciate in the manifold riches of this ancient tradition.

The thinkers assembled here, including ancient and modern Jewish men and women, range from philosophers to poets, from sages to scientists, and from playwrights to pundits. Their words provide a link with the past, and their lessons are about how to live a good life, in the most fundamental sense of the word "good." A theme underscoring the wisdom within these pages is that of balance and introspection: in the words of Rabbi Philip S. Bernstein, "always the confronting of man's weaknesses with his potentialities, always the practical instruments for living the good life, for returning to God."

Tradition! is an anthology of Jewish wisdom, past and present, that provides enduring inspiration for the future.

—S. S. Z.

ROSH HASHANAH

*T*he first holiday on the Jewish calendar, Rosh Hashanah celebrates the New Year and ushers in the Ten Days of Penitence, which conclude on Yom Kippur.

On Rosh Hashanah it is written, and on Yom Kippur it is sealed, how many shall leave this world, and how many shall be born into it, who shall live and who shall die, who shall live out the limit of his days and who shall not, who shall perish by fire and who by water . . . who shall be at peace and who shall be tormented. . . . But penitence, prayer, and good deeds can annul the severity of the decree.

—Rosh Hashanah Liturgy

Renew us for a year that is good and sweet.

—Rosh Hashanah Liturgy

Days are scrolls: write on them only what you want remembered.

–Bachya Ibn Pakuda,
11th Century

In the seventh month, on the first day of the month, you shall observe complete rest, a holy day commemorated with loud blasts.

–Leviticus 23:24

Happy the people who know the trumpet sound; these walk, O Lord, in the light of Thy face.

–Psalms 89:16

GOD and FAITH

GOD

Hear, O Israel! The Lord is our God,
the Lord is one.

–Deuteronomy 6:4

Do you know where the Lord is to be found?
He is in the place where He is invited to enter.

–Hasidic Saying

Judaism has a central, unique and tremendous
idea that is utterly original—the idea that God
and man are partners in the world and that,
for the realization of His plan and the complete
articulation of this glory upon earth,
God needs a committed, dedicated group
of men and women.

–T. H. Gaster

God is not static being, but dynamic becoming.
Without human participation, God remains
incomplete, unrealized. It is up to us to
actualize the divine potential in the world.
God needs us.

–Daniel C. Matt

A religious man is a person who holds God and
man in one thought at one time, at all times,
who suffers harm done to others, whose greatest
passion is compassion, whose greatest strength
is love and defiance of despair.

—Abraham Joshua Heschel

It hath been told thee, O men, what is good,
And what the Lord doth require of thee:
Only to do justly, and to love mercy,
and to walk humbly with thy God.

—Micah 6:8

A conviction, akin to religious feeling, of the
rationality or intelligibility of the world lies
behind all scientific work of a higher order.
This firm belief, a belief bound up with deep
feeling, in a superior mind that reveals itself
in the world of experience, represents my
conception of God.

—Albert Einstein

Without a love of humankind
there is no love of God.

—Sholem Asch

There is a breath of God in every man, a force
lying deeper than the stratum of will, which
may be stirred to become an aspiration strong
enough to give direction and even to run
counter to all winds.

–Abraham Joshua Heschel

There is no room for God in someone
who is filled with himself.

–Ba'al Shem Tov

Praised are You, O Lord, for all the colors in the
rainbow, for eyes that are made for seeing and
for beauty that is its own excuse for being.

–Rabbi Harold Schulweis

I will continue to hold my banner aloft.
I find myself born—ay, born—into a people and
a religion. The preservation of my people must
be for a purpose, for God does nothing without
a purpose. . . . The courses of the planets are no
harder to explain than the growth of a blade of
grass. Therefore am I willing to remain a link
in the great chain.

–Cyrus Adler

FAITH

A man should believe in God through faith,
not because of miracles.

–Rabbi Nahman of Bratzlav

Whoever is happy will make others happy too.
He who has courage and faith
will never perish in misery!

–Anne Frank

Jewry is not merely a question of faith,
it is above all a question of the practice of a way
of life in a community conditioned by faith.

–Franz Kafka

The Lord decides who will ride on horseback
and who will crawl on foot.
The main thing is—hope!

–Sholom Aleichem's
Tevye the Dairyman

And there is hope for thy future, saith the Lord.

–Jeremiah 31:17

It's really a wonder that I haven't dropped all
my ideals, because they seem so absurd and
impossible to carry out. Yet I keep them,
because in spite of everything I still believe that
people are really good at heart. . . . I can feel the
sufferings of millions and yet, if I look up into
the heavens, I think that it will all come right,
that this cruelty too will end, and that peace and
tranquility will return again. In the meantime,
I must uphold my ideals, for perhaps the time
will come when I shall be able to carry them out.

—Anne Frank

Tears may linger at nightfall,
but joy comes in the morning.

—Psalms 30:6

I believe in the sun even when it is not shining.

—Rabbi Marvin Reznikoff

YOM KIPPUR

*Y*om Kippur is the Day of Atonement, on which Jews fast and pray solemnly for forgiveness of the past year's sins.

For on this day atonement shall be made for you to cleanse you of all your sins; you shall be clean. It shall be a sabbath of complete rest for you and you shall practice self-denial; it is a law for all time.

—Leviticus 16:30-31

The gates of prayer are sometimes open and sometimes locked, but the gates of repentance are always open.

—Deuteronomy Rabbah 2.7

Three things are requisite for repentance: seeing eyes, ears that hear, and an understanding heart.

—Rabbi Nahman of Bratzlav

It is not external ritual that wins forgiveness,
but inward sincerity.

—Talmud

Forgive your neighbor his wrongdoing:
Then your sins will be forgiven when you pray.
Shall one man cherish anger against another,
And yet ask healing from the Lord?
Does he have no mercy on a man like himself,
And yet pray for his own sins?

—Apocrypha

To atone is to be *at one* with God, to sink self
into the not-self, to achieve a mystic unity with
the source of being, wiping out all error and
finding peace in self-submergence.

—Isaac Goldberg

Atonement is not private and introspective only,
but also public and outgoing. It is *at-one-ment*
with humanity and history and with the God of
history, or, if you will, with that which is highest
and best in history, in the universe.

—Israel Knox

OMPASSION

If I am not for myself, who will be for me?
But if I am for myself only, what am I?
And if not now, when?

—Hillel

Rejoice not when thine enemy falleth,
And let not thy heart be glad when
he stumbleth . . .

—Proverbs 24:17

If thine enemy be hungry, give him bread to eat,
And if he be thirsty, give him water to drink . . .

—Proverbs 25:21

To be a man means to be a fellow man . . .
The respect we owe to our neighbor is not an
isolated single commandment but represents
rather the whole content of morality,
the quintessence of our duty.

—Leo Baeck

Who is mighty? He who makes of his
enemy a friend.

—Fathers According to Rabbi Nathan

First become a blessing to yourself so that
you may be a blessing to others.

—Rabbi Samson Raphael Hirsch

Despise no one, and call nothing useless, for
there is no one whose hour does not come, and
there is no thing that does not have its place.

—Ben Azzai

Let other people's dignity be as
precious to you as your own.

—Rabbi Eliezer

In a place where no one behaves like a human
being, you must strive to be human!

—Hillel

Woe to him who is alone and falls with no
companion to raise him.

–Ecclesiastes 4:10

To pull a friend from the mud,
don't hesitate to get dirty.

–Ba'al Shem Tov

Who finds a faithful friend finds a treasure.

–Apocrypha

Some of us are tough on the inside yet gentle at
heart, while others of us are the extreme
opposite. Yet all of us strive to be like the fig or
the grape which is full of only goodness and
which brings joy and sustenance to the world.

–Rabbi Judith Schindler

Forgiveness is the key to action and freedom.

–Hannah Arendt

The test of a people is how it behaves toward the old. It is easy to love children. Even tyrants and dictators make a point of being fond of children. But affection and care for the old, the incurable, the helpless, are the true gold mines of a culture.

–Abraham Joshua Heschel

Give me your tired, your poor,
Your huddled masses yearning to breathe free,
The wretched refuse of your teeming shore.
Send these, the homeless,
the tempest-tossed to me,
I lift my lamp beside the golden door.

–Emma Lazarus
Engraved on the Statue of Liberty,
in NY Harbor

When we are dead, and people weep for us and grieve, let it be because we touched their lives with beauty and simplicity. Let it not be said that life was good to us, but, rather, that we were good to life.

–Jacob P. Rudin

SUKKOTH

*L*asting eight days, Sukkoth is a festival of the Autumn harvest. Meals are eaten outdoors in sukkahs, or booths, to recall the temporary shelters that the Israelites lived in as they wandered through the wilderness.

Thank you, God, for these beautiful and
fragrant fruits of the harvest, for the sun and
the rain which make them grow, for the seasons
of nature and the seasons of our lives.

—Blessing over the Lulav and Etrog

We are commanded to adorn the sukkah.
And what better ornament can there be than
the distribution of charity among those who
lack the means wherewith to be glad in the
"season of rejoicing?"

—Hayim Halberstam

Whoever is confident that God has created every
stalk of rye and every drop of water, tastes the
flavor of Paradise in everything he eats or
drinks.

—Isaac Bashevis Singer

The sukkah provides a corrective to the natural tendency of becoming excessively attached to turf. It instructs Jews not to become overly rooted, particularly not in the exile. For thousands of years Jews built homes in the Diaspora, and civilizations of extraordinary richness . . . were created. But, outside of Israel, all such Jewish homes and civilizations have proven thus far to be temporary ones, blown away when a turn of the wheel brought new forces to power. Often, self-deception and the desire to claim permanent roots led Jews to deny what was happening until it was too late to escape.

–Irving Greenberg

The sukkah is designed to teach a man to put his trust in heaven, for as he sees the universe which God created, he is inspired to trust in Him.

–Menorat Ha'maor, Chapter 3

It is necessary for you to rejoice within the sukkah and to show a cheerful countenance to guests. It is forbidden to harbor thoughts of gloom, and how much more so feelings of anger within the sukkah, the symbol of joy.

–Zohar

Torah *and* Prayer

We have preserved the Book, and the Book
has preserved us.

–David Ben Gurion

If a man looks upon the Torah as merely a book
presenting narratives and everyday matters, alas
for him! Such a Torah, one treating with
everyday concerns, and indeed a more excellent
one, we too, even we, could compile. . . . But the
Torah, in all of its words, holds supernal truths
and sublime secrets.

–Zohar

The Torah is not only a symbol of our past and
our present but a call to the future.

–Rabbi David Hachen

There are halls in the heavens above that open
but to the voice of song.

–Zohar

Prayer does not affect God but ourselves. In prayer the divine within us asserts itself, seeks its union with the divine in the universe, and through that becomes ennobled and glorified.

—*Rabbi Julius Greenstone*

The Ba'al Shem Tov said: The first time an event occurs in nature it is called a miracle; later it comes to seem natural and is taken for granted. Let your worship and your service be your miracle each day. Only such worship, performed from the heart with the enthusiasm of fresh wonder, is acceptable.

—*Hasidic, 18th Century*

Judaism is a theology of the common deed, of the trivialities of life, dealing not so much with training for the exceptional as with management of the trivial. The predominant feature in the Jewish pattern of life is unassuming, inconspicuous piety rather than extravagance, mortification, asceticism. Thus, the purpose seems to be to ennoble the common.

—*Abraham Joshua Heschel*

HANUKAH

*H*anukah is the Festival of Lights, which commemorates the victorious revolt of the Maccabees and the rededication of the Temple in Jerusalem. The celebration lasts eight days, recalling the miracle of a small cruse of oil that burned for that period of time.

Let there be light.

—Genesis 1:3

For centuries the Menorah burned constantly.
In its light a nation walked,
By its inspiration a people lived.

—Paul Romanoff

A great miracle happened there.

—Message of the Dreidel

And so they kept the dedication of
the altar eight days.

—I Maccabees 4:59

What's the best holiday? Hanukah, of course. . . .
You eat pancakes everyday, spin your dreidel
to your heart's content and from all sides money
comes pouring in. What holiday can be
better than that?

—*Sholem Aleichem*

Hanukah and St. Nicholas Day came almost
together this year—just one day's difference.
We didn't make much fuss about Hanukah:
we just gave each other a few little presents
and then we had the candles. Because of the
shortage of candles we only had them alight
for ten minutes, but it is all right as
long as you have the song.

—*Anne Frank*

Yours the message cheering
That the time is nearing
Which will see
All men free,
Tyrants disappearing.

—*Mo'oz Tzur, Rock of Ages
The Hanukah Hymn*

$\mathscr{K}$NOWLEDGE

Who is truly wise?
One who learns from all people.

—Pirke Avot 4:1

The beginning of wisdom is to desire it.

—Solomon Ibn Gabirol

Get wisdom;
Yea, with all thy getting get understanding.

—Proverbs 4:7

The pursuit of knowledge for its own sake, an
almost fanatical love of justice, and the desire
for personal independence, these are the
features of the Jewish tradition which make me
thank my lucky stars I belong to it.

—Albert Einstein

Increase your knowledge,
or you will decrease it!

—Mishnah

The Divine test of a person's worth
is not theology but life.

—Talmud

Be diligent in study. To learn below your
potential is a betrayal of self and an insult to life.

—Rabbi Judah

The wise man should be generous in imparting
his knowledge to others.
For knowledge is not lessened in the giving.

—Solomon Ibn Gabirol

Wisdom consists in the highest use of the
intellect for the discernment of the largest moral
interest of humanity. It is the most perfect
willingness to do the right combined with the
utmost attainable knowledge of what is right. . . .
Wisdom consists in working for the better from
the love of the best.

—Felix Adler

Nurture your mind with great thoughts.
To believe in the heroic makes heroes.

—Benjamin Disraeli

Teach thy tongue to say, "I do not know."

—Proverb

Knowledge by itself is insufficient.
It must also penetrate the heart.

—Rabbi Israel Salanter

PURIM

*P*urim is the Feast of Lots, which celebrates the deliverance of the Persian Jews from a massacre. On Purim, Jews wear costumes and the day is marked by parties and merrymaking.

Make them days of feasting and gladness, and of sending portions one to another, and gifts to the poor.

—Talmud

And it was so, when the king saw Esther the queen standing in the court, that she obtained favor in his sight: and the king held out to Esther the golden scepter that was in his hand.

—Esther 5:2

Purim [is] a time to feel good and to let loose, a time to masquerade as someone other than yourself. The spirit of Purim is best captured in the Talmudic dictum "It is the obligation of each person to be so drunk [on Purim] as not to be able to tell the difference between 'Blessed be Mordechai' and 'Cursed be Haman.'"

—Michael Strassfeld

FAMILY, HOME, and LOVE

FAMILY

Be fruitful, and multiply,
and replenish the earth.

–Genesis 1:28

Now the Lord said unto Abram: . . .
I will bless thee, and make thy name great;
and be thou a blessing. And I will bless them
that bless thee, and . . . in thee shall all
the families of the earth be blessed.

–Genesis 12:1-3

Our God and God of our fathers, preserve
this child to his father and to his mother . . .
Let the father rejoice in his offspring, and the
mother be glad with the fruit of her body . . .
This little child, may he become great.
Even as he has entered into the covenant,
so may he enter into the Torah, the nuptial
canopy, and into good deeds.

–Prayer Book

Train up a child in the way he should go, and even when he is old, he will not depart from it.

–Proverbs 22:6

Fruits take after their roots.

–Abraham Ibn Ezra

[Daddy] said: "All children must look after their own upbringing." Parents can only give good advice or put them on the right paths, but the final forming of a person's character lies in their own hands.

–Anne Frank

The Jewish mother . . . is the inspirer of a . . . family life whose hallowing influences are incalculable: she is the center of all spiritual endeavors, the confidante and fosterer of every undertaking. To her the Talmudic sentence applies: "It is women alone through whom God's blessings are vouchsafed to a house."

–Henrietta Szold

God could not be everywhere, so He created mothers.

–Leopold Kompert

HOME

First a person should put his house together,
then his town, then the world.

–Rabbi Israel Salanter

The center of Judaism is in the home. . . .
it is at home where the essential celebrations
and acts of observance take place—rather than
in the synagogue or temple . . . The synagogue
is an auxiliary . . . A Jewish home is where
Judaism is at home, where Jewish learning,
commitment, sensitivity to values are
cultivated and cherished.

–Abraham Joshua Heschel

If you know you're going home,
the trip is never too hard.

–Chofetz Chaim

The Jew's home has rarely been his "castle."
Throughout the ages it has been something
far higher—his sanctuary.

–J. H. Hertz

LOVE

God said, "It is not good for man to be alone."

–*Genesis 2:18*

Many waters cannot quench love.
Neither can the floods drown it . . .

–*The Song of Songs 8:7*

Sex has never been considered a sin. . . .
Sex has always been considered a blessing. . . .
Somebody just told me when he has sex
he actually sees angels.

–*Dr. Ruth Westheimer*

In expressing love we belong among the
undeveloped countries.

–*Saul Bellow*

If you want to know about a man you can find
out an awful lot by looking at who he married.

–*Kirk Douglas*

Success in marriage does not come merely
through finding the right mate, but through
being the right mate.

–Rabbi Barnett R. Brickner

As together you now drink from this cup,
So may you, under God's guidance,
In perfect union and devotion to each other,
Draw contentment, comfort and felicity
From the cup of life;
Thereby may you find life's joys
doubly gladdening,
Its bitterness sweetened,
And all things hallowed
By true companionship and love.

–The Marriage Ritual

I am my beloved's, and my beloved is mine.

–The Song of Songs 6:3

PASSOVER

*P*assover, or Pesah, celebrates the exodus of the Jews from bondage in Egypt. On Passover, ceremonial meals called seders are held in Jewish households the world over.

Let My people go.

—Exodus 5:1

And you shall explain to your child on that day,
"It is because of what the Lord did for me when
I went free from Egypt."

—Exodus 13:8

The Passover affirms the great truth that liberty
is the inalienable right of every human being.
The Feast of Israel's freedom, its celebration
is Israel's homage to the great principle of
human freedom.

—Morris Joseph

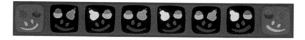

We are commanded to recall the past, in order to remember the *present*—to see it clearly, to know it fully, in all its possibilities—in the light of our future redemption. We . . . look back in order to look forward: We thus come to see that we also stand *among* redemptions—acts of freedom, births of possibility—that we might not have seen, or assisted in, without the paradigm of Pesah.

—Arnold Eisen

The seder is really not about the re-experiencing of the slavery and redemption of the Hebrews. . . .We all have our own Egypt to leave . . . It is not a re-experience, which cannot really be, but an experience. It is not theater but life.

—Edward L. Greenstein

Abraham Joshua Heschel was fond of saying that the important thing in life is to ask the right questions. For this we need an occasion, a structure, a set of symbols to prod us, all of which are provided by the sensory delights of the seder table.

—Arnold Eisen

All of us are equal, and though you are poor you will not feel estranged at my table, for all of us were impoverished in Egyptian bondage.

—Don Isaac Abrabanel

All who are hungry, let them come and eat.

—Passover Haggadah

And a stranger shalt thou not oppress: for ye know the heart of a stranger, seeing ye were strangers in the land of Egypt.

—Exodus 23:9

By the rivers of Babylon, there we sat down, yea, we wept, when we remembered Zion. . . . For there they that carried us away captive required of us a song. . . . How shall we sing the Lord's song in a strange land?

—Psalms 137:1, 3-4

Our people retained its uniqueness in Egypt.
They did not alter their way of life, their
convictions, their names, their heritage, their
faith, their language. By virtue of this self-
respect and dignity they merited redemption.

−Don Isaac Abrabanel

I am a Jew because, born of Israel and having
lost her, I have felt her live again in me, more
loving than myself.

−Edmond Fleg

This night is different because we celebrate the
most important moment in the history of our
people. On this night we celebrate their going
forth in triumph from slavery into freedom.

−Leon Uris

CHARITY AND ETHICS

CHARITY

For there will never cease to be needy ones in
your land, which is why I command you:
open your hand to the poor and needy.

—Deuteronomy 15:11

A person should be more concerned with
spiritual than with material matters,
but another person's material welfare
is his own spiritual concern.

—Rabbi Israel Salanter

When a person begs for food and clothing,
there must be no investigation of his need,
for we are told: "When thou seest the
naked . . . cover him."

—Talmud

The only way of converting darkness into light
is by giving to the poor.

—Shneur Zalman

When it comes to giving Tzedakah,
there are four kinds of personalities:
One who wants to give,
but doesn't want others to—
he resents the Mitzvah-work of others.
One who wants others to give,
but not himself—
he is greedy.
One who wants to give,
and that others should also give—
he is saintly.
One who doesn't want to give,
and doesn't want others to give either—
he is downright wicked.

—Sayings of the Fathers 5:16

The noblest of all charities is in enabling the
poor to earn a livelihood.

—Proverb

Through faith we experience the meaning of the
world; through action we give the world
meaning.

—Rabbi Leo Baeck

ETHICS

The purpose of man's life is not happiness,
but worthiness.

—Felix Adler

Keep far from falsehood.

—Exodus 23:7

Neither shall you allege the example of the
many as an excuse for doing wrong.

—Exodus 23:2

The first requisite of civilization . . .
is that of justice.

—Sigmund Freud

Enter not into the path of the wicked,
And walk not in the way of evil men.
Avoid it, pass not by it;
Turn from it, and pass on.

—Proverbs 4:14-15

Man has been given free will: if he wishes to turn toward the good way and to be righteous, the power is in his own hands; if he wishes to turn toward the evil way and to be wicked, the power likewise is in his own hand.

—*Maimonides*

Man's understanding of what is right and wrong has often varied throughout the ages; yet the consciousness that there is a distinction between right and wrong is permanent and universal.

—*Abraham Joshua Heschel*

A half truth is a whole lie.

—*Yiddish Proverb*

A liar's punishment is that even when he tells the truth, he is not believed.

—*Talmud*

One should never conduct his affairs with
smooth talk and false flattery. Nor may one say
one thing and mean another. A man's inner
intentions must correspond to his outer actions;
his mouth must express his inner thoughts.

—Maimonides

At first sin is like a spider's web; in the end it
becomes as thick as a ship's cable. At first it is
a visitor; in the end it becomes the
master of the house.

—Midrash

The evil impulse is sweet in the beginning and
bitter in the end.

—Jerusalem Talmud 14:3

Let a good man do good deeds with the same
zeal that the evil man does bad ones.

*—Hasidic saying attributed to the Belzer Rebbe,
Shalom Rokeakh*

To hurt innocent people whom I knew many
years ago in order to save myself is, to me,
inhuman and indecent and dishonorable. I
cannot and will not cut my conscience to fit this
year's fashions.

–*Lillian Hellman*

Light is sown for the righteous,
And gladness for the upright in heart.

–*Psalms 97:11*

SHAVUOT

*S*havuot is the Feast of Weeks, an agricultural festival which traditionally commemorates the receiving of the Ten Commandments.

And thou shalt observe the feast of weeks, even of the first-fruits of wheat harvest, and the feast of ingathering at the turn of the year.

–Exodus 34:22

The Torah is a tree of life to those who hold fast to it, and all who cling to it find happiness.

–Proverbs 3:18

Turn it (the Torah) again and again, for everything is in it.

–Avot 2:8

1. I am the Lord your God who brought you out of the land of Egypt, the house of bondage.

2. You shall have no other gods besides Me.

3. You shall not carry the Lord your God's name in vain.

4. Remember the Sabbath day to make it holy.

5. Honor your father and mother.

6. You shall not murder.

7. You shall not commit adultery.

8. You shall not steal.

9. You shall not bear false witness against your neighbor.

10. You shall not covet your neighbor's house; you shall not covet your neighbor's wife, or . . . anything that is your neighbor's.

–The Ten Commandments, Exodus 20:2-14

ISTORY AND PEACE

HISTORY

Jews fix our years by the moon, other nations by
the sun. Those who depend on the sun are
strong and fight for their survival and existence
as long as fortune shines on them, but as soon as
their sun sets, they vanish from the pages of
history. Not so the People of Israel who live on
and shine during the darkest stretches of the
night, just like the moon, that sends forth its
light in the night's darkest hours.

—Aryeh Leib

Judaism is rooted forever in the soil, blood, life-
experience and memory of a particular folk—
the Jewish people.

—Solomon Goldman

A race that persists in celebrating their vintage,
although they have no fruits to gather, will
regain their vineyards.

—Benjamin Disraeli

Memory is a passion no less powerful or
pervasive than love. What does it mean to
remember? It is to live more than one world, to
prevent the past from fading and to call upon
the future to illuminate it. It is to revive
fragments of existence, to rescue lost beings, to
cast harsh light on faces and events, to drive
back the sands that cover the surface of things.

—*Elie Wiesel*

We have survived persecution because of the
virtues and sacrifices of our ancestors.

—*Louis D. Brandeis*

Recently at a public banquet I happened to sit
next to a lady who tried to impress me by
vouchsafing the information that one of her
ancestors witnessed the signing of the
Declaration of Independence. I could not resist
replying: "Mine were present at the Giving of
the Ten Commandments."

—*Stephen S. Wise*

We are God's stake in human history. We are the
dawn and the dusk, the challenge and the test.

—*Abraham Joshua Heschel*

PEACE

No man can think clearly when
his fists are clenched.

–George Jean Nathan

A leader who doesn't hesitate before he sends
his nation into battle is not fit to be a leader.

–Golda Meir

When we are trying to decide whether a leader
is a good leader or a bad one, the question to
ask is: "Is he with the Ten Commandments or is
he against them?" Then you can determine if
the leader is a true messiah or another Stalin.

–Isaac Bashevis Singer

Men and nations behave wisely once they
have exhausted all other alternatives.

–Abba Eban

Struggle is the law of life. Must we not fight, all of us, even for the peace that we most crave?

−Louis D. Brandeis

When you have two views, you don't have to become two peoples. We are one people. . . . We recognize the right of the opposition to oppose us, to change the government. But we expect the opposition to make our nation free and democratic, having many views, and to remain together.

−Shimon Peres

There is no doubt whatsoever in my mind that the risks of peace are preferable by far to the grim certainties that await every nation in war.

−Yitzhak Rabin

Peace will come, despite the opponents of peace.

−Leah Rabin

SABBATH

*I*n accordance with God's will, Jews observe the Sabbath from sundown on Friday to sundown on Saturday. The Sabbath is hallowed to recall that God rested on the seventh day, after creating the world in six days.

Six days you shall labor, and do all your work,
but the seventh day is a Sabbath of the Lord,
and that day you shall not work, neither you,
nor your son or daughter, nor any of your
servants, nor your cattle, nor the stranger that is
within your gates.

–Exodus 20:9-10

The Sabbath is scented with the perfume of
Paradise. As it reaches earth, sorrow and sighing
flee away. Peace and joy reign supreme.

–Zohar

The meaning of the Sabbath is to celebrate time rather than space. Six days a week we live under the tyranny of things in space; on the Sabbath we try to become attuned to *holiness in time.* It is a day when we are called upon to share in what is eternal in time, to turn from the results of creation to the mysteries of creation; from the world of creation to the creation of the world.

–*Abraham Joshua Heschel*

Far more than Israel has kept the Sabbath, it is the Sabbath that has kept Israel.

–*Achad Ha'am*